French - Portuguese

LEARNING FLASHCARDS

FOR BABIES TODDLERS

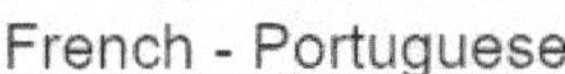

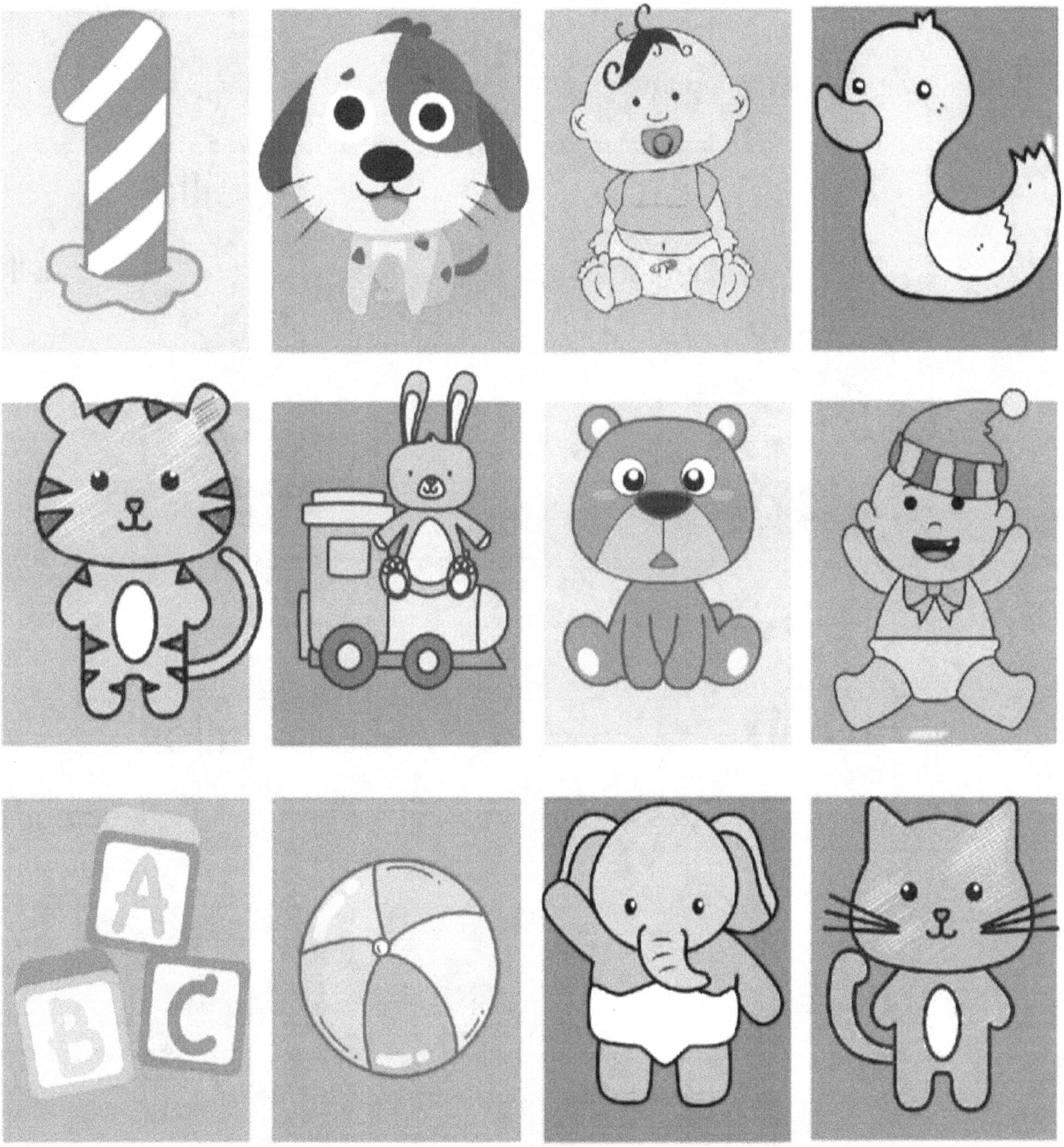

alligator

jacaré

The alligator is having a party.

fourmi

formiga

The ant is red.

ours

urso

The bear loves you.

abeille

abelha

The bee is saying hello.

oiseau

pássaro

The bird is flying.

papillon

borboleta

The butterfly is pretty.

chameau

camelo

The camel has a hump.

chat

gato

The cat is happy.

dinosaure

dinossauro

The dinosaur is laying eggs.

poulet

frango

The chicken is dancing.

vache

vaca

The cow has a bell.

cerf

veado

The reindeer has a toy.

chien

cão

The dog has two floppy ears.

dauphin

golfinho

The dolphin is swimming.

canard

pato

The duck has a bow.

aigle

águia

The eagle is looking for food.

l'éléphant

elefante

The elephant is sitting.

poisson

peixe

The fish is a clownfish.

libellule

libélula

The dragonfly is blue.

renard

raposa

The fox has a red nose.

grenouille

rã

The frog is smiling.

girafe

girafa

The giraffe has a long neck.

chèvre

bode

The goat has a beard

ver de terre

minhoca

The worm is in the apple

poule

galinha

The hen has chicks.

hippopotame

hipopótamo

The hippo is big.

cheval

cavalo

The horse is fast.

kangourou

canguru

The kangaroo has a baby.

chaton

gatinho

The kitten is playing.

lion

leão

The lion has a mane.

homard

lagosta

The lobster is red.

singe

macaco

The monkey has a tail.

poulpe

polvo

The octopus has food.

hibou

coruja

The owls have big eyes.

panda

panda

The panda wears a diaper.

porc

porco

The pig is fat and pink.

chiot

cachorro

The dog is brown.

lapin

coelho

The rabbit has a carrot.

rat

rato

The mouse is writing something.

crabe

caranguejo

The crab has two pinchers.

requin

tubarão

The shark is scary.

mouton

ovelha

The sheep are very fluffy.

escargot

caracol

The snail is slow.

serpent

serpente

The snake has poison.

araignée

aranha

The spider is purple.

écureuil

esquilo

The squirrel has a nut.

tigre

tigre

The tiger has a red bow.

tortue

tartaruga

The turtle has a shell.

loup

lobo

The wolf is smiling.

zèbre

zebra

The zebra is black and white.

dinde

peru

The turkey has two legs.

coq

galo

The rooster will crow.

perroquet

papagaio

The parrot is colorful.

hérisson

ouriço

The hedgehog has apples.

pomme

maçã

The apple has a leaf.

abricot

damasco

The apricot is yellow.

avocat

abacate

The avocado has a nut.

banane

banana

The banana is yellow.

la mûre

amora

There are a lot of blackberries.

cassis

groselha preta

The blackcurrants are yummy.

myrtille

mirtilo

The blueberries are sweet.

cerise

cereja

The cherries have a stem.

noix de coco

coco

The coconuts have juice.

figues

figos

The fig has seeds.

grain de raisin

uva

The grapes are purple.

pamplemousse

toranja

The grapefruits are sour.

kiwi

kiwi

The kiwi is fresh.

citron

limão

The lemons are yellow.

citron vert

lima

We have lots of lime.

litchi

lichia

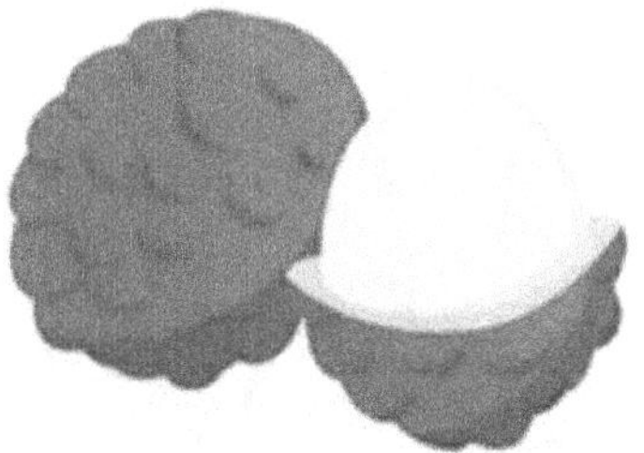

I like to eat lychee.

mandarine

tangerina

Oranges are refreshing.

mangue

manga

Mango is my favorite fruit.

orange

laranja

Mandarins are like oranges.

papaye

mamão

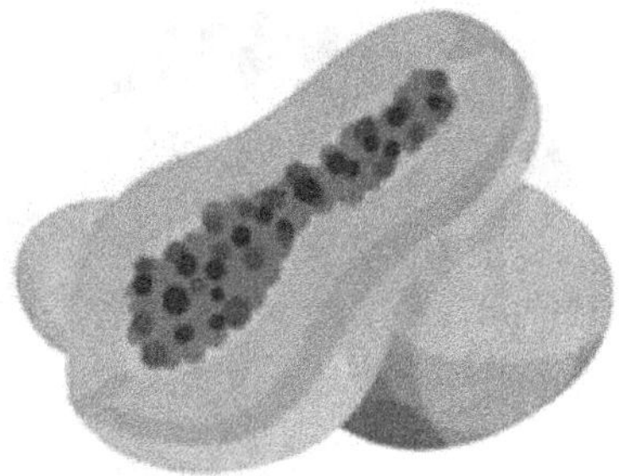

Papayas have lots of seeds.

pêche

pêssego

Peaches are juicy.

poire

pera

Pears have a strange figure.

ananas

abacaxi

The pineapple has a thumbs up.

prune

ameixa

Plums are healthy for you.

grenade

roma

Pomegranates are all red.

framboise

framboesa

The raspberry is shiny.

fraise

morango

The strawberry has leaves on top.

pastèque

melancia

The watermelon is big.

mandarine

tangerina

The tangerine looks like an orange.

tarte

torta

I like to eat apple pie.

gâteau

bolo

That cake is huge.

bonbons

doce

Candy is not good for your teeth.

biscuit

biscoito

Cookies are easy to make.

donut

rosquinha

I like strawberry donuts.

crème glacée

sorvete

The ice cream is melting.

muffin

bolinho

The muffin has a cute wrapper.

pudding

pudim

We eat pudding on Christmas.

classeur

encadernador

I keep pictures in my binder.

livre

livro

I like to eat books.

sac à dos

mochila

The backpack has lots of stuff.

les ciseaux

tesouras

I have scissors in my bag.

épingles

pinos

Pins can hold stuff up.

agrafe

grampo

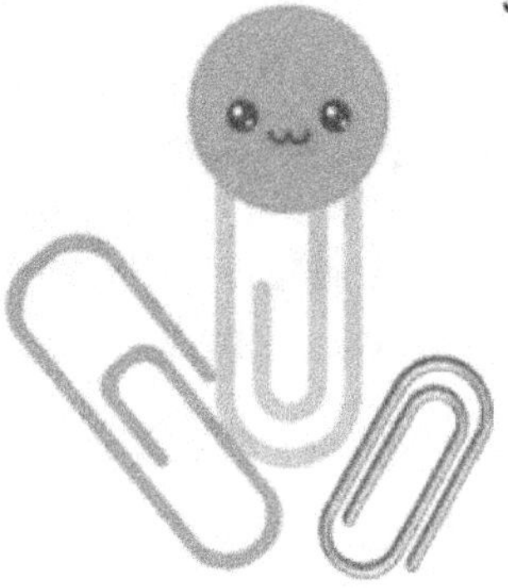

Clips can hold up paper.

papier

papel

I have lots of paper.

agrafeuse

agrafador

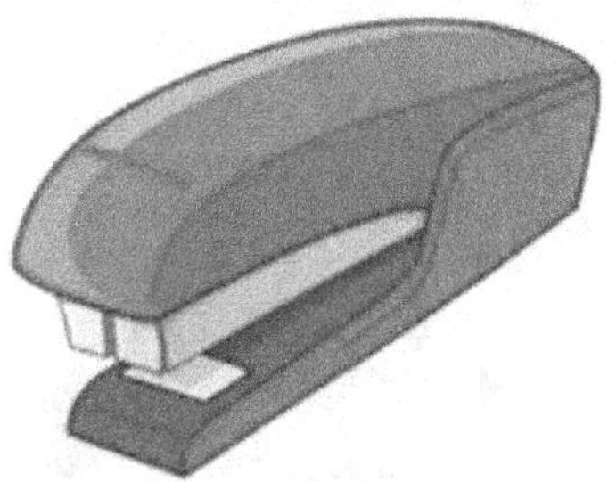

My stapler is shiny and red.

calculatrice

calculadora

My calculator has buttons.

règle

governante

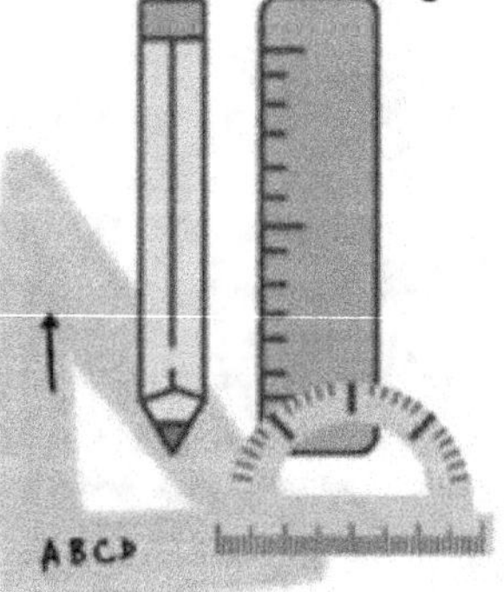

I have lots of rulers.

la colle

cola

The glue is sticky.

bibliothèque

estante

My bookcase has lots of things.

calendrier

calendário

I have a calendar on my table.

chaise

cadeira

My chair is fancy.

l'horloge

relógio

The clock says that it's 3 o'clock.

ordinateur

computador

I do things on my computer.

bureaux

mesas

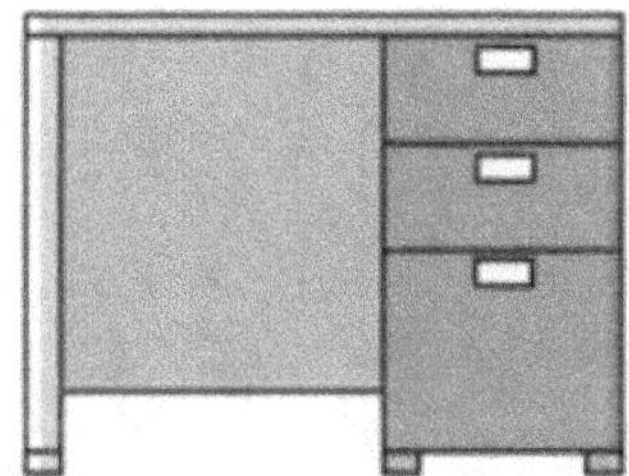

I put lots of things on my desk.

dictionnaire

dicionário

The dictionary has lots of words.

la gomme

apagador

Erasers are used with pencils.

carte

mapa

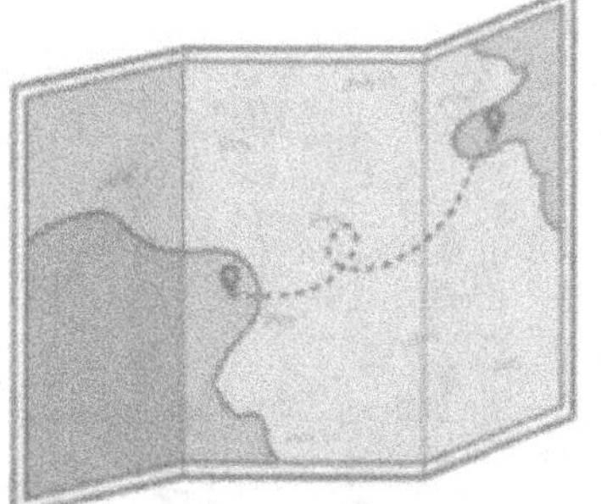

The map shows you different places.

carnet

caderno

I use notebooks at school.

stylo

caneta

My pen is very pretty.

crayon

lápis

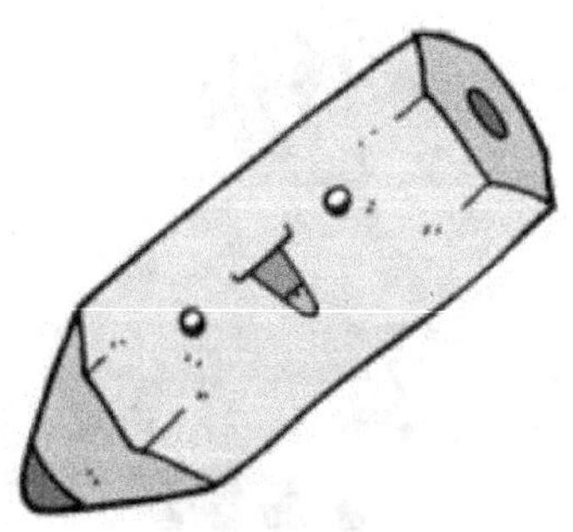

My friend gave me a pencil.

ceinture

cinto

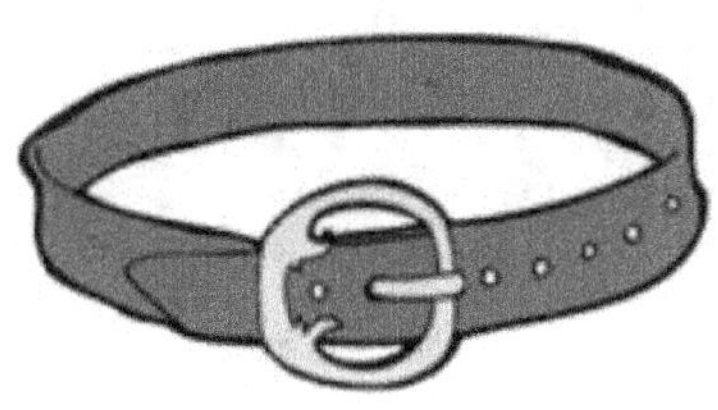

I have a belt on my pants.

bottes

chuteiras

I have big brown boots.

chapeau

chapéu

My mom bought me a new cap.

manteau

casaco

She has a long yellow coat.

robes

vestidos

My dress has a bow.

gants

luvas

I got new gloves.

chapeau

chapéu

That hat is for a wicked witch.

veste

jaqueta

The jacket is cozy.

jeans

jeans

My jeans are long.

pyjamas

pijamas

I sleep in my pajamas.

un pantalon

calça

The bear is wearing pants.

imperméable

capa de chuva

We wear our raincoats when it is raining.

écharpe

cachecol

The baby has a scarf around his neck.

chemise

camisa

I like this shirt the best.

des chaussures

sapatos

I have red and blue shoes.

jupe

saia

My skirt has lots of buttons.

pantalon

calças

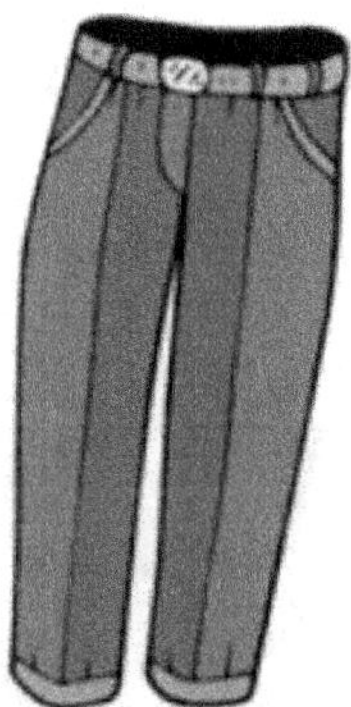

My dad wears slacks.

chaussons

chinelos

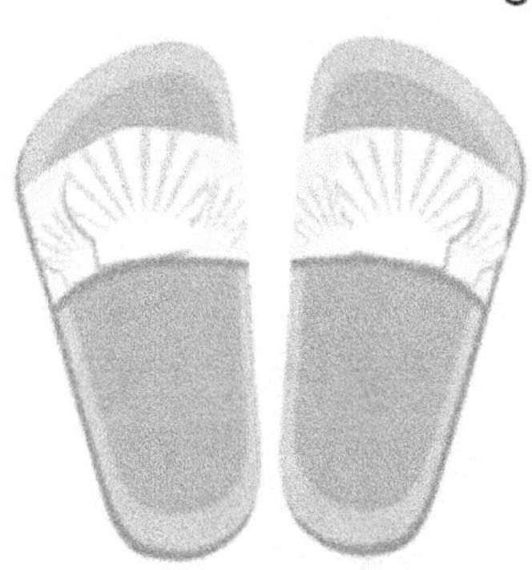

I have seashells on my sandals.

chaussettes

meias

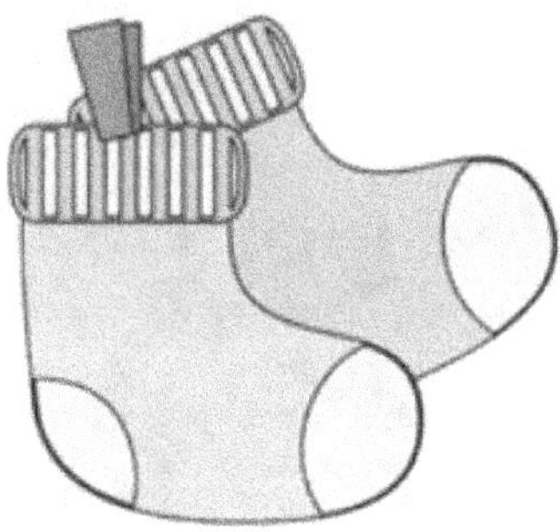

My baby sister wears socks.

costume

terno

My brother is wearing a suit.

chandail

suéter

I am wearing a sweater for winter.

cravate

gravata

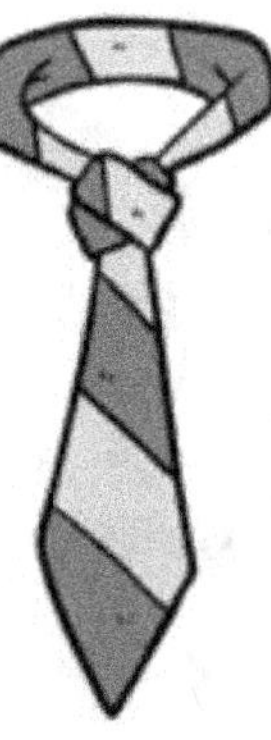

My dad wears a tie to meetings.

pantalon

calças

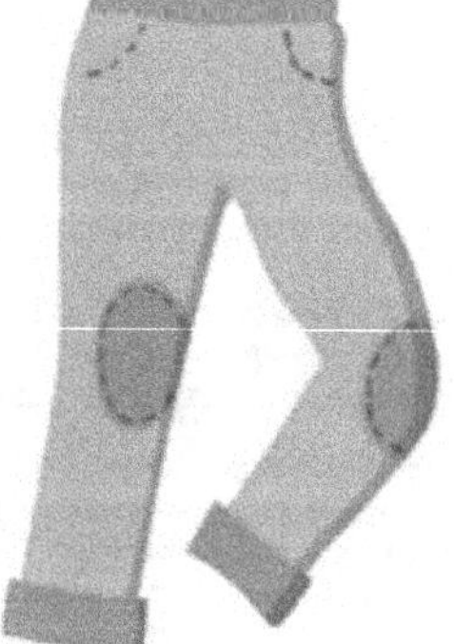

The trousers look like jeans.

slip

cuecas

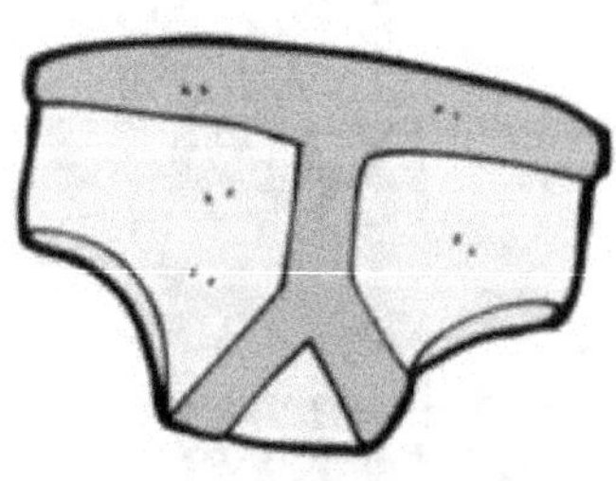

I always wear my underwear.

maillot de corps

camisola

My undershirt has a star.

une

1

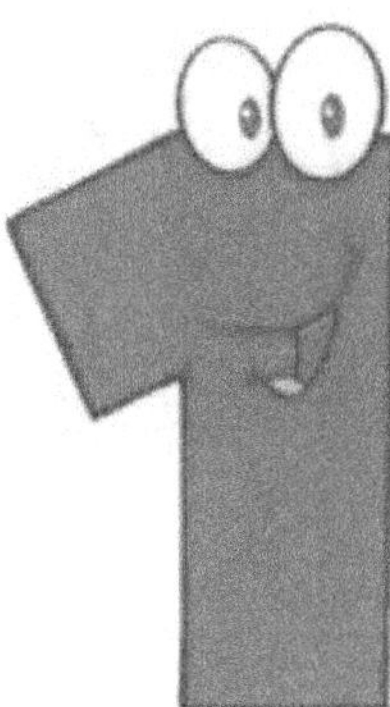

Number one and the bee are friends.

deux

dois

The cat and the mouse both love two.

trois

três

The bear gives number three a present.

quatre

quatro

Number four is a home for the cat.

cinq

cinco

Number five hatches an egg.

six

seis

Number six is going to eat a carrot.

sept

sete

Number seven is playing with the tiger.

huit

oito

Number eight is funny.

neuf

nove

Number nine meets the parrot.

dix

dez

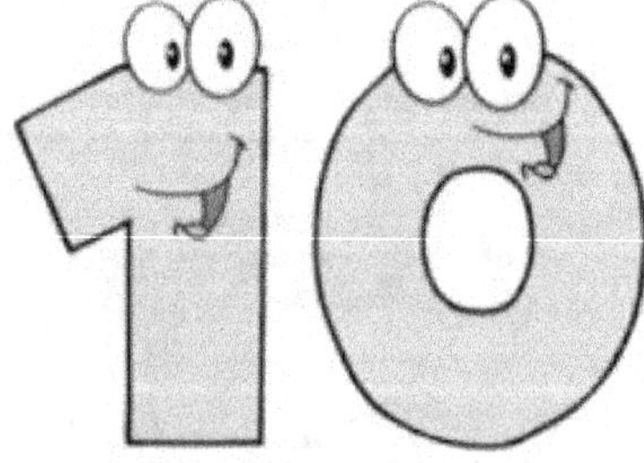

Number ten is smiling.

onze

onze

Number eleven has big eyes.

douze

doze

Number twelve is number one and two.

treize

treze

Number thirteen is excited.

quatorze

quatorze

The number fourteen is vast.

quinze

quinze

The number fifteen is green.

seize

dezesseis

Sixteen is my lucky number.

dix-sept

dezessete

Number seventeen look alike.

dix-huit

dezoito

Number eighteen will go to the circus.

dix-neuf

dezenove

I am nineteen now!

vingt

vinte

Number twenty has a zero.

fourmi

formiga

The ant has lots of legs.

cloche

sino

The bell will ring.

vache

vaca

The cow has a bow.

poupée

boneca

She has a cute bear doll.

oeuf

ovo

The chick has hatched out of the egg.

poisson

peixe

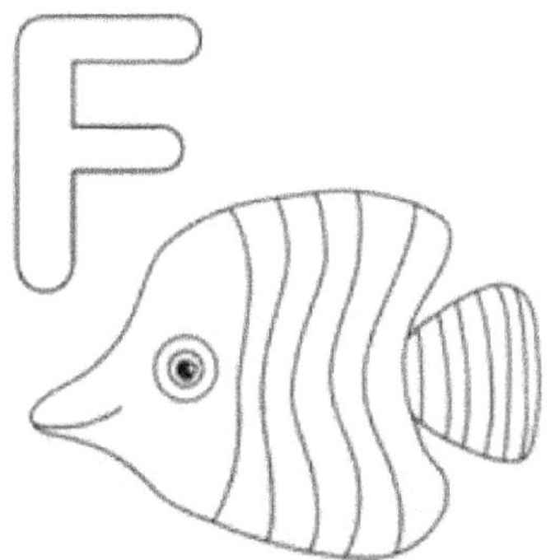

The fish is swimming in the water.

chèvre

bode

The goat is sitting on the grass.

chapeau

chapéu

He is wearing a hat.

crème glacée

sorvete

I like to eat ice cream.

confiture

geléia

The kitten is sitting on the jam jar.

chaton

gatinho

The cat is sleeping on the floor.

lion

leão

The lion is waiting for the tiger.

rat

rato

The mouse has lots of presents.

nez

nariz

The reindeer has a red nose.

hibou

coruja

The owl is sleeping.

porc

porco

The pig will eat cupcakes.

reine

rainha

The queen has a big crown.

lapin

coelho

The rabbit is jumping up and down.

mouton

ovelha

The sheep have fluffy wool.

tortue

tartaruga

The turtle has a shell.

parapluie

guarda-chuva

The mouse is holding an umbrella.

van

furgão

The van is driving along the road.

pastèque

melancia

The watermelon has lots of seeds.

xylophone

xilofone

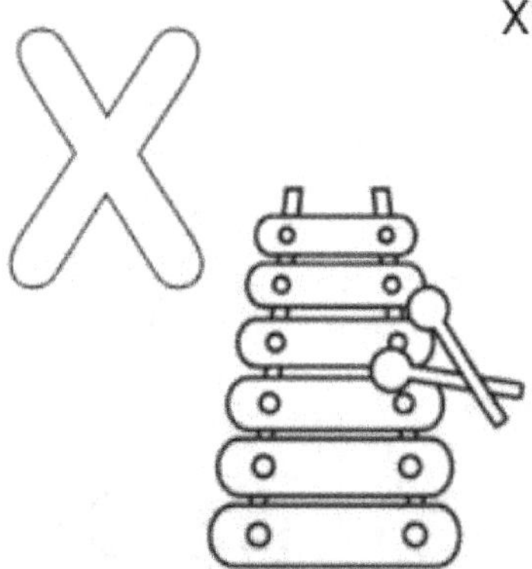

We are going to play the
xylophone.

yaourt

iogurte

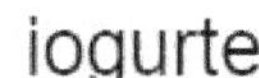

We opened the yogurt can.

zèbre

zebra

The zebra is surprised.

rose

rosa

color the word and
the picture in pink

Most of my clothes are pink.

marron

castanho

color the word and
the picture in pink

My chocolate is brown.

gris

cinzento

color the word and
the picture in pink

I don't like the color gray.

vert

verde

color the word and
the picture in pink

The vegetables are green.

jaune

amarelo

color the word and
the picture in pink

Bananas are yellow.

blanc

branco

color the word and
the picture in pink

The paper that I write on is white.

rouge

vermelho

color the word and
the picture in pink

Apples are red.

bleu

azul

color the word and
the picture in pink

The night sky is blue.

percer

broca

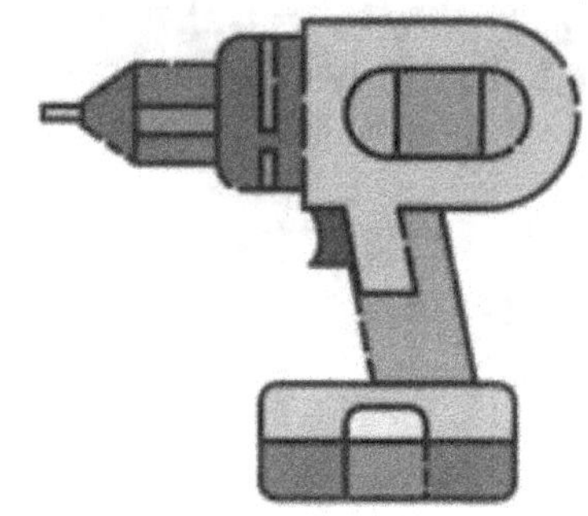

The drill will help us fix this.

marteau

martelo

The hammer is going to nail the
picture.

couteau

faca

The knife is sharp.

pinces

alicate

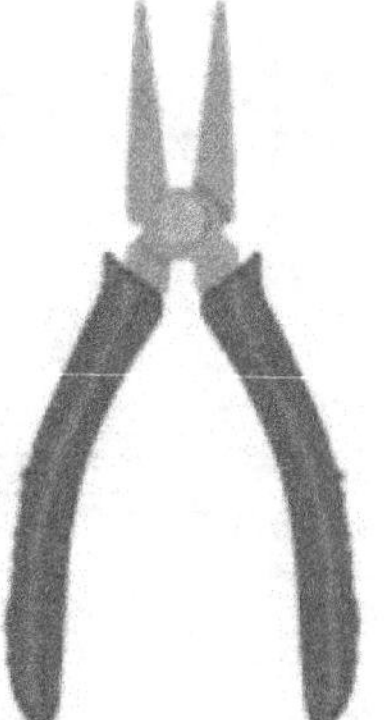

The plier is used for many things.

vu

serra

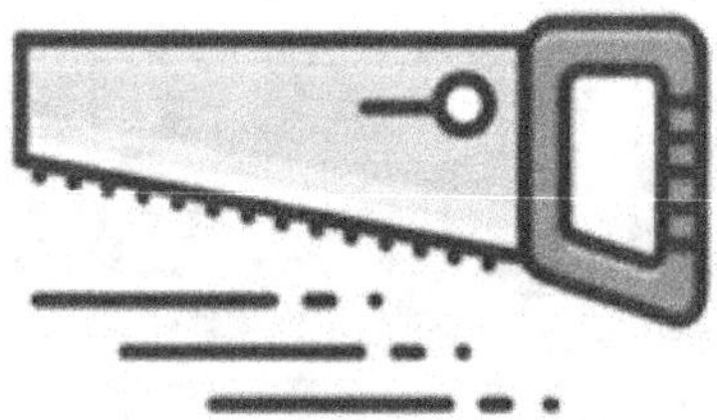

The saw can chop wood.

les ciseaux

tesouras

I use scissors to cut paper.

tournevis

chave de fenda

The screwdriver can screw in the knots.

clé

chave inglesa

The wrench can help unscrew the knots.

avion

avião

The airplane is going to leave now.

vélo

bicicleta

The bicycle is beautiful.

bateau

barco

The boat is floating on the water.

autobus

ônibus

The bus is going to school.

voiture

carro

The car is green.

hélicoptère

helicóptero

The helicopter is looking for something.

cheval

cavalo

You can ride the horse.

jet

jato

The jet is high-speed.

moto

motocicleta

The motorcycle is on the road.

navire

navio

The ship is on the water.

métro

metrô

My mom goes on the subway to work.

taxi

táxi

The taxi has someone inside.

train

trem

The train is going slowly.

un camion

caminhão

The truck has stuff in it.

asperges

espargos

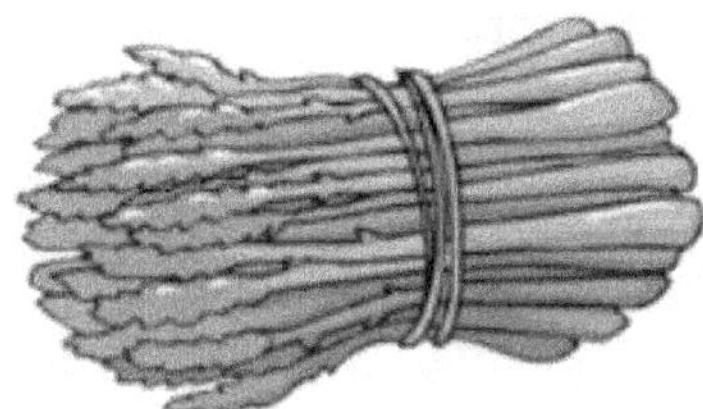

The asparagus is in a bundle.

des haricots

feijões

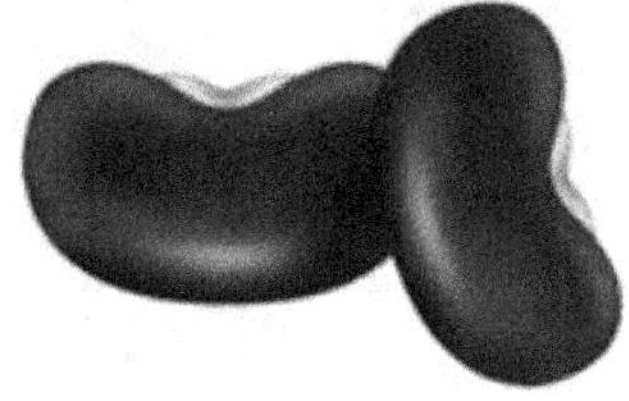

The beans are smooth.

brocoli

brócolis

The broccoli is dancing.

chou

repolho

Bunnies like to eat cabbage.

carotte

cenoura

The carrots are very long.

céleri

salsão

The celery has lots of leaves.

blé

milho

Corn soup is delicious.

concombre

pepino

The cucumbers are cut into pieces.

aubergine

berinjela

The eggplant is purple.

poivre vert

pimenta verde

The green pepper is juicy.

salade

alface

The lettuce is all green.

oignon

cebola

The onions make my eyes water.

pois

ervilhas

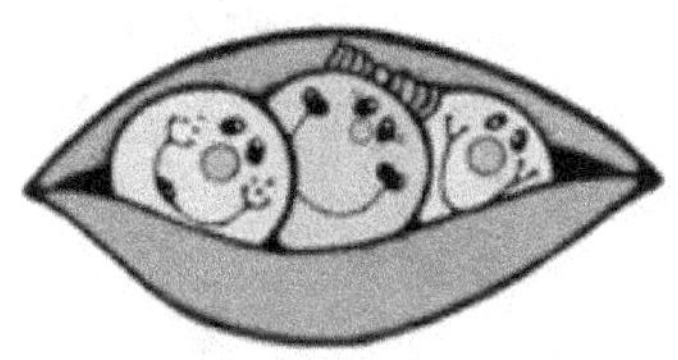

The peas are all in a pod.

patate

batata

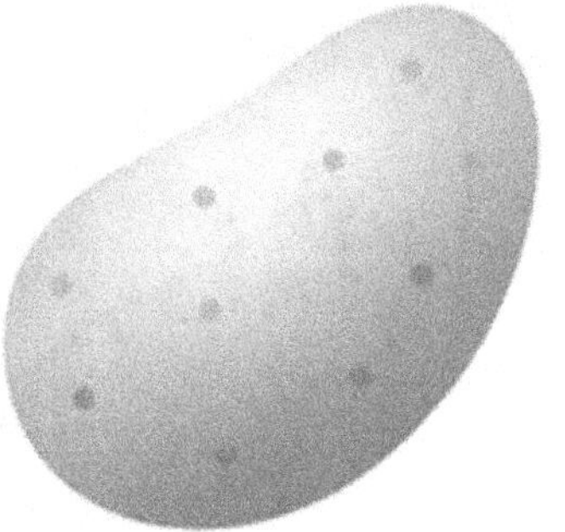

The potato is very shiny.

citrouille

abóbora

The pumpkin is for Halloween.

un radis

rabanete

The radish is a type of vegetable.

épinard

espinafre

The spinach is good with cheese.

patate douce

batata doce

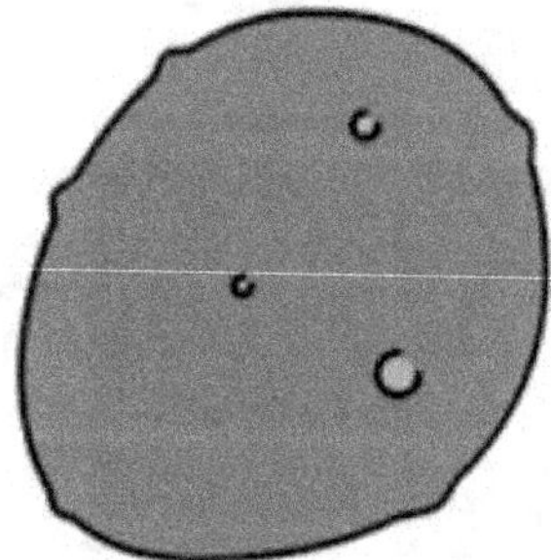

The sweet potato is quite sweet.

tomate

tomate

I don't like to eat tomatoes.

navet

nabo

My mom bought some turnips.

nuageux

nublado

The weather is cloudy today.

du froid

frio

I like cold weather.

cool

legal

The temperature is cold today.

brumeux

nebuloso

The fog is so strong I can't see the city.

chaud

quente

The fire is burning hot.

humide

úmido

It's so humid and wet today.

pluvieux

chuvoso

It's raining very hard.

neigeux

nevado

Welcome to snow land!

orageux

tormentoso

I hate the stormy weather.

ensoleillé

ensolarado

The sun is shining!

chaud

caloroso

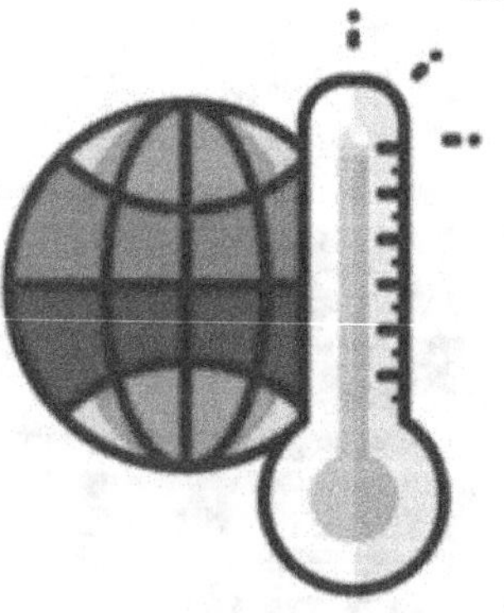

The whole world is warm today!

venteux

ventoso

The leaves are blowing away since it's so windy!

tante

tia

My aunt is very nice to me.

frère

irmão

My brother is very fun to play with.

cousin

primo

I love going to the playground with my cousin.

fille

filha

I like to read books with my daughter.

père

pai

My father is playing with me.

petite fille

neta

My granddaughter has blond hair.

grand-mère

avó

My grandmother is very old and has glasses.

petit fils

neto

My grandson and I are very excited today!

mère

mãe

My mother likes to pick me up.

neveu

sobrinho

My father's nephew is my cousin.

nièce

sobrinha

My niece is very good at playing ball.

sœur

irmã

My sister is so pretty!

fils

filho

My son likes to play with toy cars.

belle fille

enteada

My stepdaughter likes the color orange.

belle-mère

madrasta

My stepmother is pretty.

beau-fils

enteado

This is my stepson, Greg.

oncle

tio

My uncle tells lots of funny jokes.

bol

tigela

The bowl has nothing inside.

tasse

copo

My mom drinks her coffee out of a cup.

plat

prato

That dish has a bone inside.

fourchette

garfo

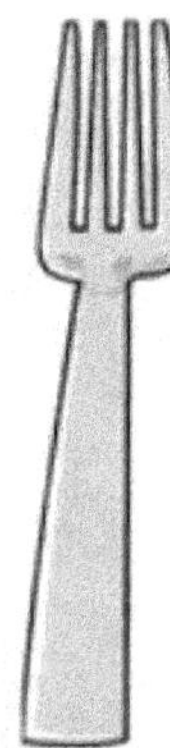

We have more spoons than forks.

verre

vidro

I have a glass of water on my desk.

couteau

faca

I have a knife in my kitchen.

agresser

caneca

This mug of coffee is for my dad.

serviette de table

guardanapo

You can use the napkins to clean your hands.

poivre

pimenta

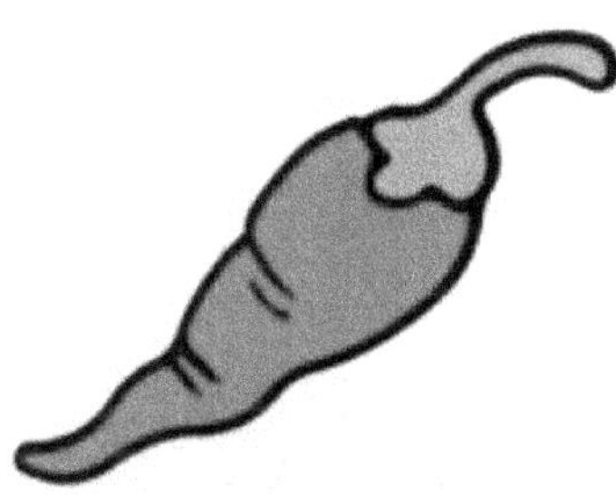

The pepper is very spicy.

lanceur

jarro

Pour yourself some lemonade from the pitcher.

assiette

prato

Can you help me wash the plates?

salade

salada

The salad is very healthy for you.

sel

sal

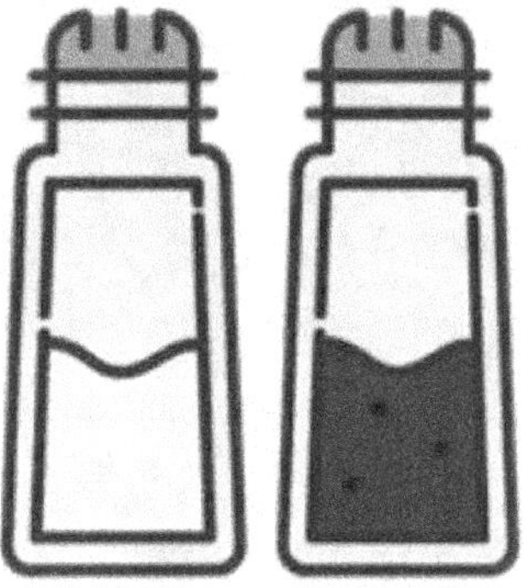

The salt tastes good with a few pinches of pepper.

soucoupe

pires

The plate is for my cup.

cuillère

colher

I use a spoon to eat my rice.

sucre

açúcar

The pack of sugar is very heavy.

dimanche

domingo

Sunday

Sunday is the day to go to Church!

lundi

segunda-feira

Monday

Monday is the day to start school.

mardi

terça

Tuesday

We will go to the shops on Tuesday.

mercredi

quarta-feira

Wednesday

Wednesday is hard to spell!

jeudi

quinta-feira

Thursday

Thursday is the fourth day of the week!

vendredi

sexta-feira

Friday

My birthday is on Friday!

samedi

sábado

Saturday

Saturday is the weekend!

cuire

assar

The chef will bake a cake.

ébullition

ferver

I will boil the eggs.

griller

assar

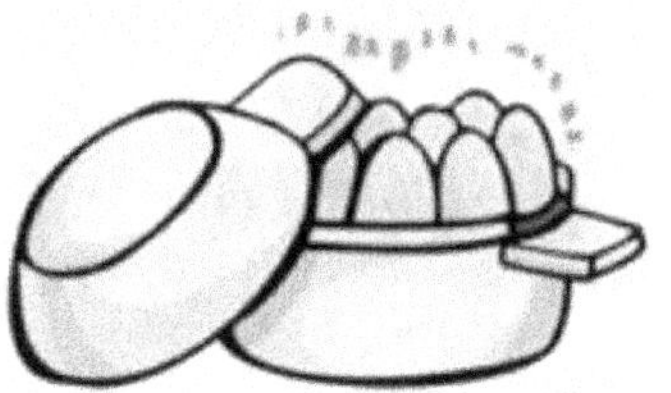

Broil is very yummy.

ouvre-boîte

abridor de lata

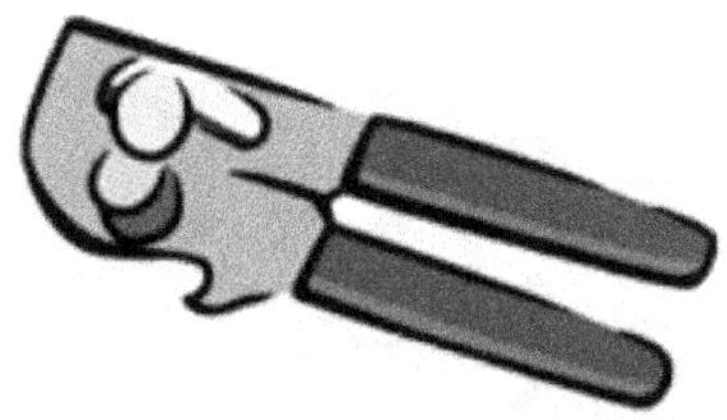

That can opener is used for opening cans.

frire

fritar

The pan can fry lots of things.

gril

grade

We have a grill in our backyard.

tasse à mesurer

copo medidor

My mom uses the measuring cup for baking.

cuillère à mesurer

colher de medida

I use a measuring spoon to eat my dessert.

four micro onde

microondas

The microwave is used to heat food.

bol à mélanger

tigela de mistura

She is using the mixing bowl to mix things.

serviettes en papier

toalhas de papel

Dry your hands with paper towels.

poché aux œufs

ovo cozido

The poach is put on noodles.

porte pot

suporte de panela

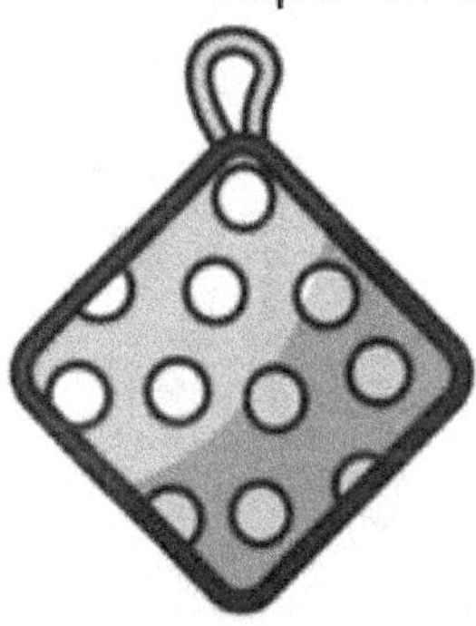

The potholder is soft.

rôti

assado

The chef made roast chicken.

rouleau à pâtisserie

rolo

He is holding a rolling pin.

brouiller

passeio

My mom is making scrambled eggs for breakfast.

mijoter

ferver

The simmer is rice today.

couteau

faca

The knife is sharp.

cuillère

colher

I eat my food with a spoon and fork.

spatule

espátula

The spatula will help us flip the steak over.

vapeur

vapor

The steam is coming from the pot.

passoire

filtro

The strainer is used to strain stuff.

minuteur

cronômetro

I set my timer for 12:00.

fourchette

garfo

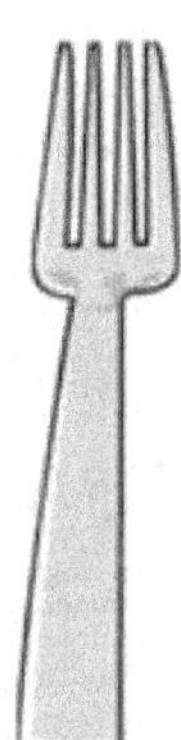

I have lots of metallic forks.

grille-pain

torradeira

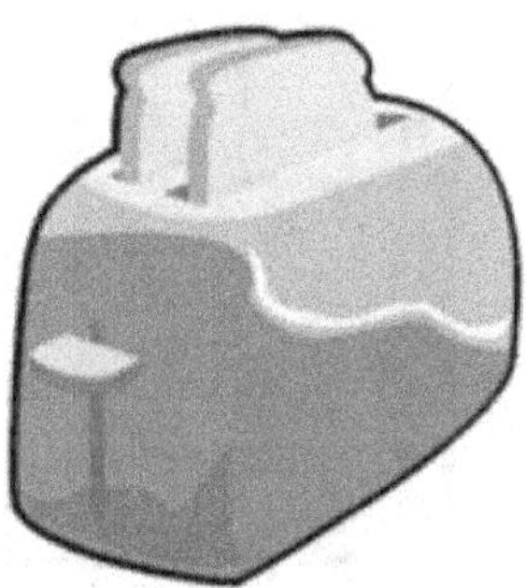

The toaster will toast my bread.

bouilloire

chaleira

The kettle has tea inside.

réfrigérateur

frigorífico

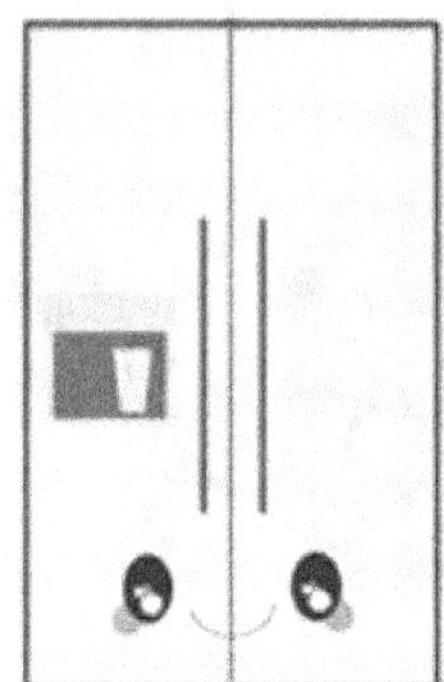

The refrigerator has lots of things inside.

mixeur

liquidificador

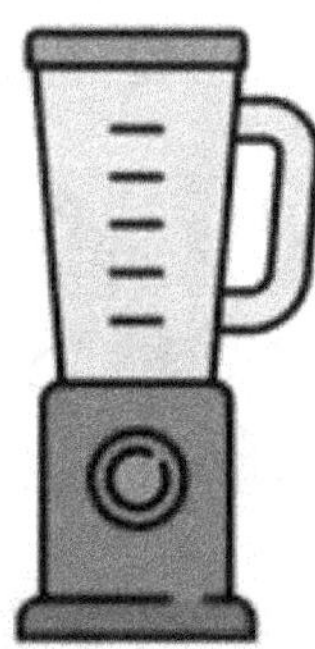

The blender will mix up my fruits.

cabinets

armários

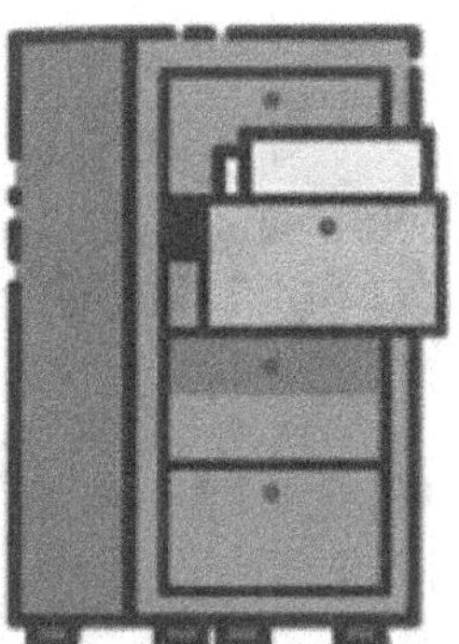

The cabinet has my paper inside.

placard

armário

The cupboard has lots of books.

four micro onde

microondas

The microwave will heat my food.

arrière

costas

She has a slender back.

des joues

bochechas

She kisses her mom on the cheek.

poitrine

peito

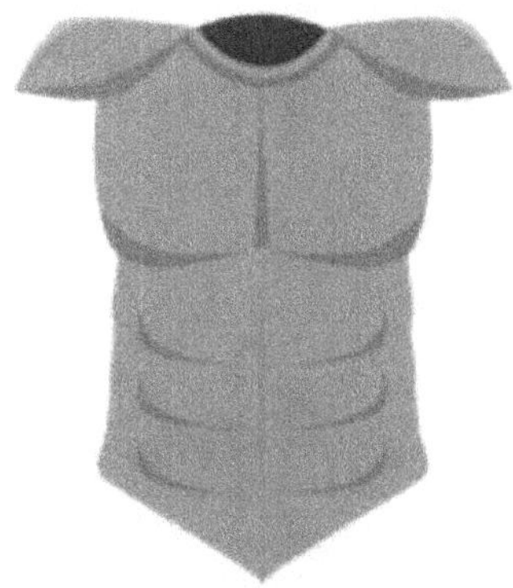

The armor is for your chest.

menton

queixo

This is my chin!

oreilles

orelhas

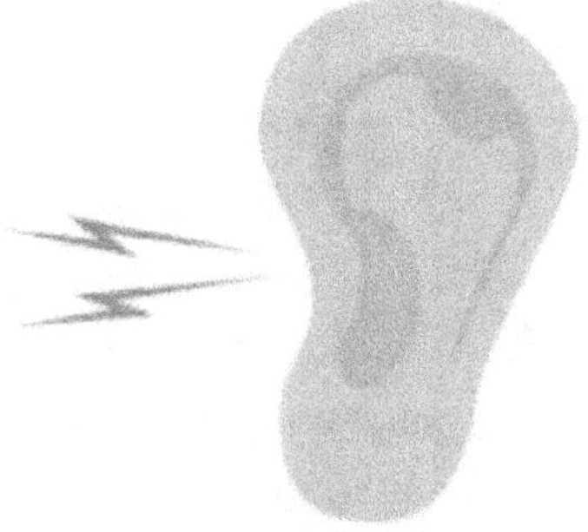

The ear is hearing something.

les sourcils

sobrancelhas

The eyebrows are raised.

yeux

olhos

The eyes are blue.

pieds

pés

I have one pair of feet.

des doigts

dedos

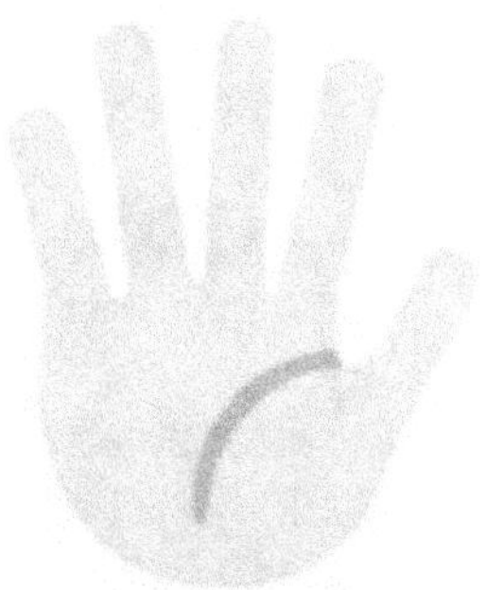

The fingers are waving at us.

pied

pé

My foot has five fingers.

front

testa

My brain is behind my forehead.

cheveux

cabelo

My hair is long and black.

mains

mãos

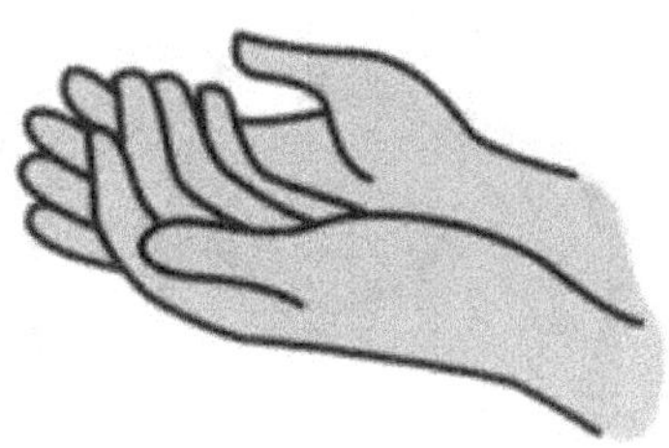

I will wash my hands in the sink.

tête

cabeça

She has a big head.

les hanches

ancas

The gorilla has his hands on his hips.

les genoux

joelhos

She is begging on her knees.

jambes

pernas

The tiger has strong legs.

lèvres

lábios

The lips have lipstick on.

bouche

boca

He is covering his mouth with his hand.

cou

pescoço

The necklace is very special to me.

nez

nariz

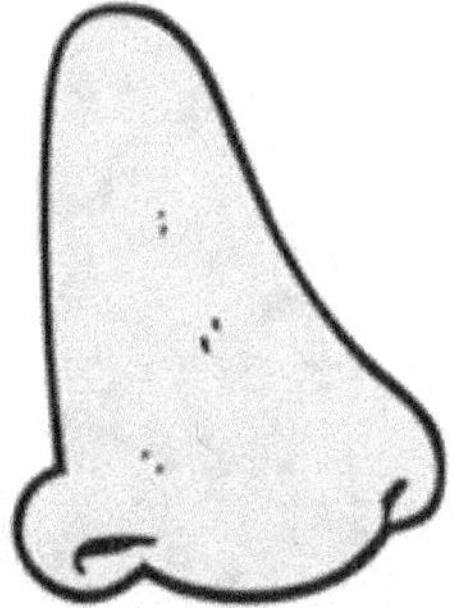

The nose smells something.

épaules

ombros

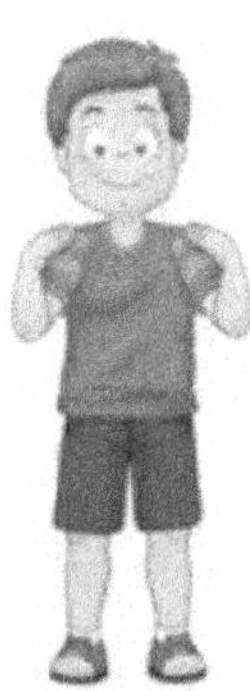

He puts his hands on his shoulders.

estomac

estômago

He has a big stomach.

les dents

dentes

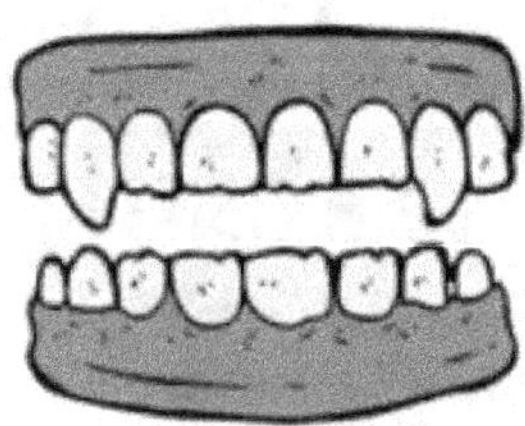

The teeth are clean and white.

gorge

garganta

He has a sore throat today.

les orteils

dedos do pé

My toes are small.

langue

língua

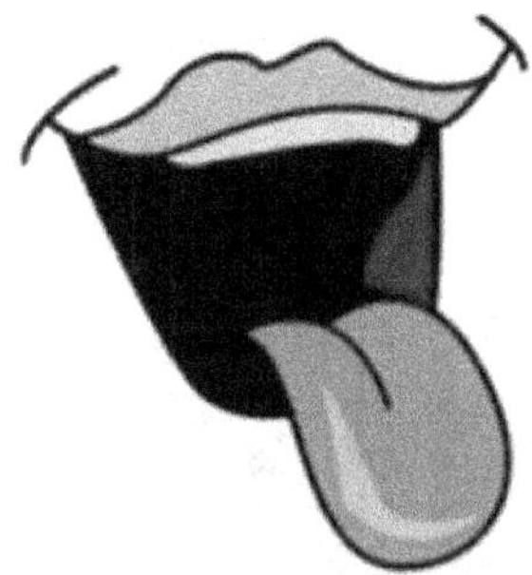

My tongue is licking ice cream.

dent

dente

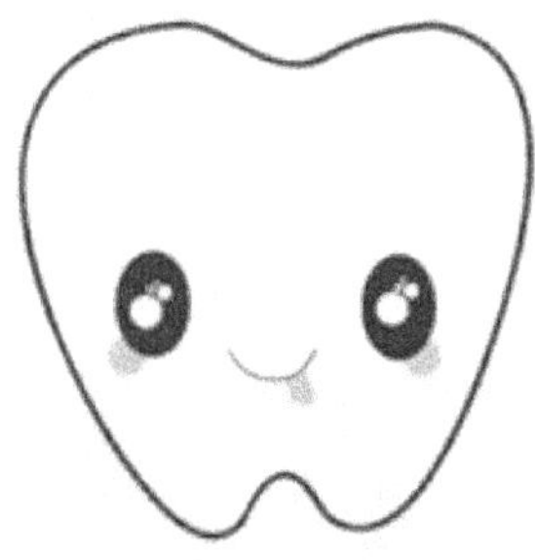

The tooth has big eyes.

taille

cintura

He has his hands on his waist.

salopette

macacão

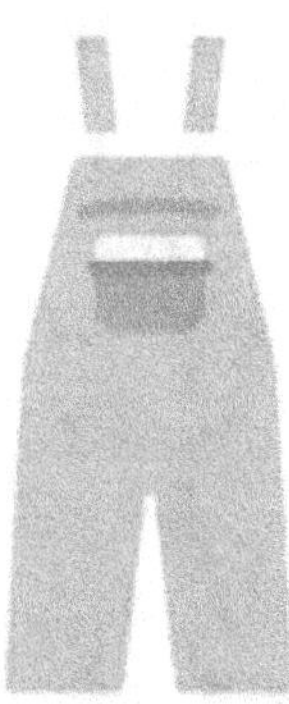

I bought these overalls for you!

mitaines

luvas

The mittens are very warm.

bonnet

gorro

The beanie is for winter.

tablier

avental

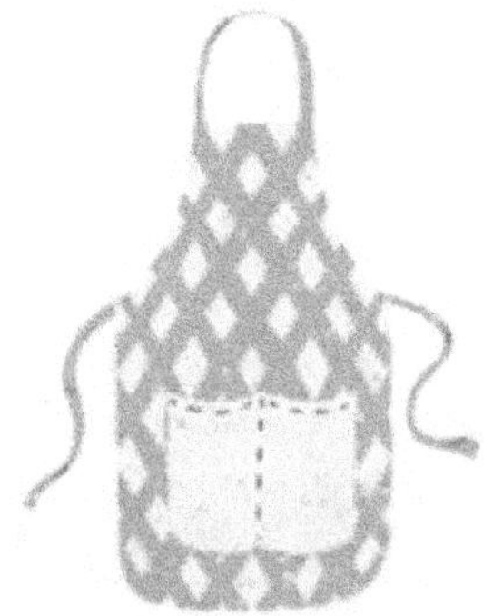

I wear my apron when I bake.

poupée

boneca

The doll is for my baby sister.

hochets

chocalhos

The rattle is for the baby.

jouet

brinquedo

The toy is very fun.

couche

fralda

The baby has to wear a diaper.

berceau

berço

She is sleeping in her bassinet.

bavoir

babador

My baby brother has to wear his
bib when he is eating.

octogone

octógono

The octagon is saying okay!

triangle

triângulo

The triangle has three corners.

carré

quadrado

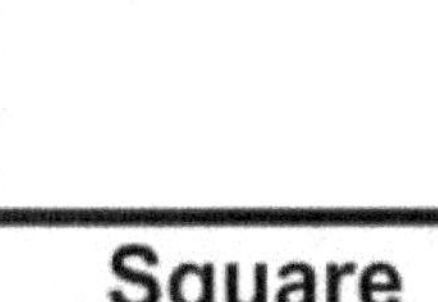

Square

The square has four sides.

cercle

círculo

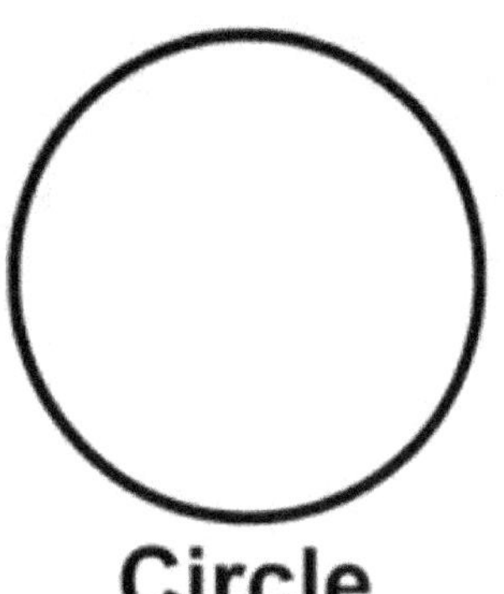

Circle

The circle is round.

ovale

oval

The oval shape looks like a circle.

cœur

coração

I drew a heart on my paper.

traverser

cruz

That sign is a cross.

la flèche

seta

The arrow is pointing this way.

cube

cubo

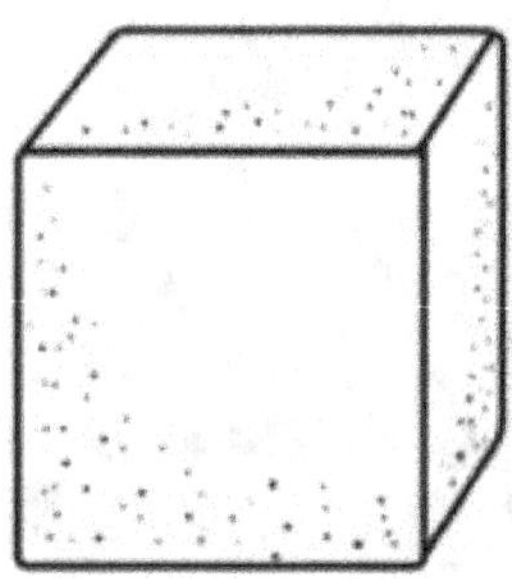

The cube is 3D.

étoile

estrela

The star is yellow and shiny.

tir à l'arc

tiro com arco

The archery is where you aim.

badminton

badminton

My favorite sport is badminton.

criquet

grilo

I am very good at cricket.

bowling

boliche

I got one pin down at bowling!

boxe

boxe

The boxing gloves are hot.

tennis

tênis

He can hit the ball in tennis.

faire de la planche à roulettes

skate

He skateboards to school.

planche de surf

prancha de surf

The shark loves surfing in the ocean.

le hockey

hóquei

I like to play Ice hockey.

yoga

ioga

He is closing his eyes and doing yoga.

épée

esgrima

They are fencing and dueling together.

aptitude

ginástica

She will do some fitness in the pool.

gymnastique

ginástica

He can do brilliant gymnastics.

karaté

karatê

She is good at kicking in Karate.

volley-ball

vôlei

She is holding a volleyball.

musculation

levantamento de peso

The girl with brown hair can do weightlifting.

basketball

basquetebol

He can balance the ball with one finger in basketball.

base-ball

basebol

The little chick is in the finales at baseball.

le rugby

rugby

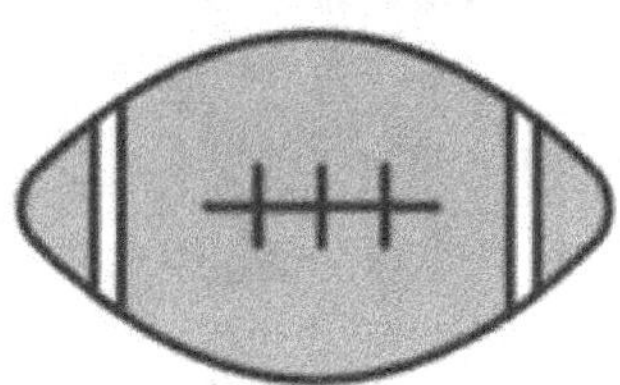

The rugby ball has white stripes.

lutte

luta livre

The sumo will compete in wrestling.

course de voitures

corridas de carros

He is number one for car racing.

cyclisme

ciclismo

He is peacefully cycling on the road.

fonctionnement

corrida

He is running while listening to his earphones.

tennis de table

tênis de mesa

My brother and dad will play table tennis.

pêche

pescaria

He will go to the river to fish.

judo

judo

She has a red belt in Judo.

escalade

escalada

He will climb the ladder.

tournage

tiroteio

He is shooting the archery board.

le golf

golfe

She is going to compete in the golf competition.

balade

passeio

He will ride his scooter.

asseyez-vous

sentar-se

They are sitting down together.

se lever

levante-se

She likes to stand up.

bats toi

luta

They are fighting over the book.

rire

rir

He is laughing so hard!

lis

ler

She read a picture book.

jouer

jogar

He went to play on the slide.

ecoutez

ouço

He listened for the ice cream cart.

pleurer

chorar

He cried because he got a bad grade.

pense

pensar

He thought that the test would be hard.

chanter

cantar

He sang for the concert.

regarder la télévision

assistir tv

He watched TV the whole night.

danse

dança

She was a good dancer.

allumer

ligar

The light is turned on.

éteindre

desligar

The light is turned off.

gagner

ganhar

He won the contest.

mouche

voar

The parrot can fly.

couper

cortar

He was cutting his nails.

désinvolte

jogar fora

He threw away the garbage.

dormir

dormir

He slept soundly.

fermer

perto

He closed his mouth shut.

ouvert

abrir

She opened the bathroom door.

écrire

escrever

She wrote with a pencil.

donner

dar

Santa gave her a present.

sauter

saltar

She had fun jumping.

manger

comer

The shark ate yummy ice cream.

boisson

bebida

The old British man drank tea.

cuisinier

cozinhar

The microwave cooked his soup.

lavage

lavar

You need to remember to wash your hands.

attendre

esperar

He was waiting for the bus.

montée

escalar

She climbed a lot of mountains.

parler

falar

Two best friends were talking together.

crawl

rastejar

The baby crawled on the floor.

rêver

sonhe

The Sloth dreamed about eating leaves.

creuser

escavação

That strong man dug a swimming pool.

taper

aplaudir

The baby clapped her hands.

tricoter

malha

She knits with the purple string.

coudre

costurar

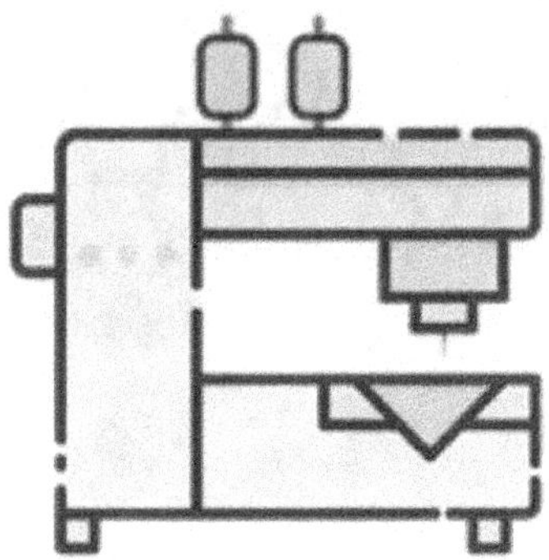

That is a sewing machine.

odeur

cheiro

The perfume smelled great.

baiser

beijo

He kissed his mother.

étreinte

abraço

They hugged each other.

ronfler

ronco

The tiger snored.

baigner

banhar-se

He took a bath.

s'incliner

curvando-se

He bowed to the judge.

peindre

pintura

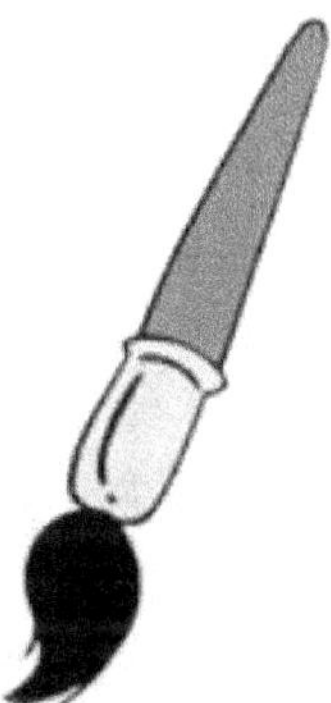

He painted a colorful picture.

se plonger

mergulho

He dove to the deepest part of the ocean.

ski

esqui

The ski was expensive.

empiler

pilha

The books are stacked high.

acheter

comprar

They bought cereal.

secouer

mexe

They shook hands together.

programmeur

programador

He was a smart computer programmer.

vétérinaire

veterinário

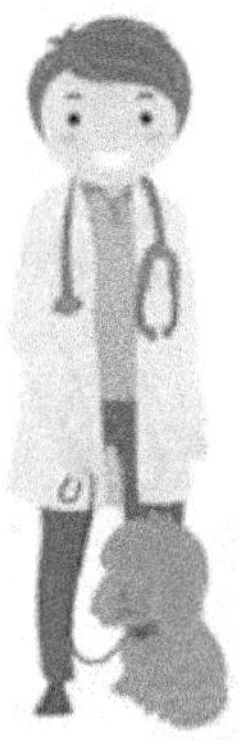

She is a veterinarian.

vendeur de rue

vendedor de rua

That street vendor sells hot dogs.

mineur

mineiro

That Miner will find gold.

prof

professor

The owl is the teacher.

groom

mensageiro de hotel

That Bellboy is fat.

orateur

alto falante

The chicken is a great Speaker.

boucher

açougueiro

The Butcher sells fish.

pharmacien

farmacêutico

That Pharmacist saved a person's life.

réceptionniste

recepcionista

He is a Receptionist.

politicien

político

He wants to be a Politician.

guide touristique

guia turístico

That Tour guide led us around Japan.

entrepreneur

empreendedor

He is an Entrepreneur.

danseuse de ballet

bailarina

She is training to be a Ballet dancer.

astronaute

astronauta

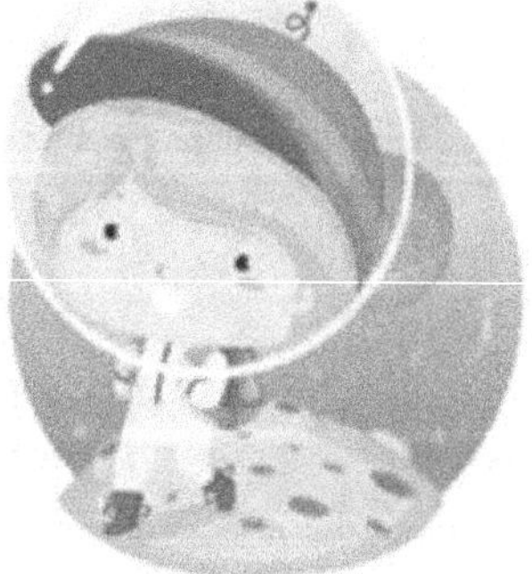

He is a great astronaut.

juge

juiz

That Judge is always fair.

avocat

advogado

The lawyer is serious.

la caissière

caixa

She is a cashier at the market.

conducteur de taxi

taxista

He is a fast Taxi driver.

plombier

encanador

That Plumber fixes toilets.

musicien

músico

She wants to be a Musician like her teacher.

chef

chefe de cozinha

The chef makes fast food.

boulanger

padeiro

That baker is a bread.

artiste

artista

That Artist came from Italy.

acteur

ator

That actor is famous.

barman

barkeeper

The Bartender works in a bar.

coiffeur

cabeleireiro

That girl is a Hairdresser.

évêques

bispos

He is a Bishop.

opticien

oculista

She went to an Optician.

fleuriste

florista

She is a great Florist.

écrivain

escritor

He is a famous author.

comptable

contador

My accountant is loyal.

du vin

vinho

That wine tastes good.

café

café

That coffee is bitter.

limonade

limonada

The lemonade is refreshing.

chocolat chaud

chocolate quente

I drink hot chocolate every day.

milk-shake

milkshake

The milkshake has whipped cream.

eau

água

The water is not cold.

thé

chá

The tea is hot.

lait

leite

Milk is white.

bière

cerveja

The beer is foamy.

un soda

refrigerante

The soda is fizzy.

smoothie

smoothie

The smoothie is a watermelon flavor.

milk-shake

milkshake

The milkshake has whipped cream.

lait de coco

leite de côco

The coconut milk is yummy.

du jus d'orange

suco de laranja

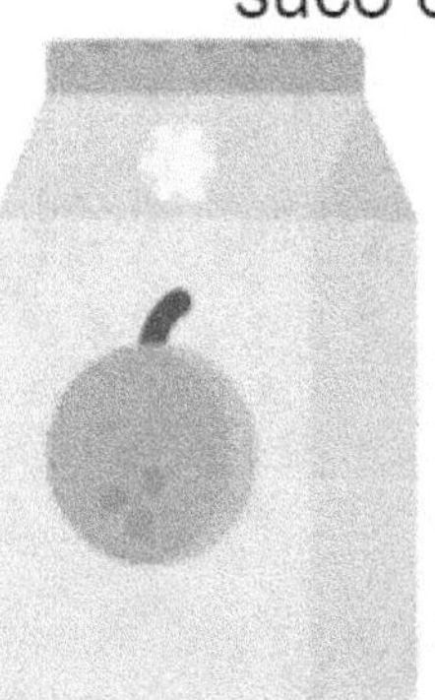

The orange juice is made from oranges.

cacao

cacau

The cocoa is sweet.

fromage

queijo

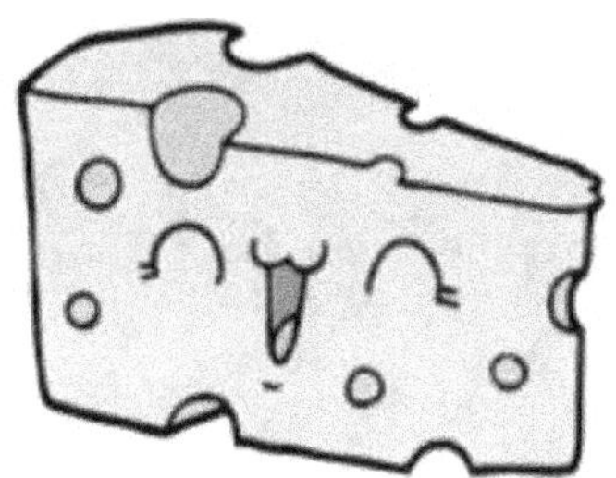

The cheese is creamy.

oeuf

ovo

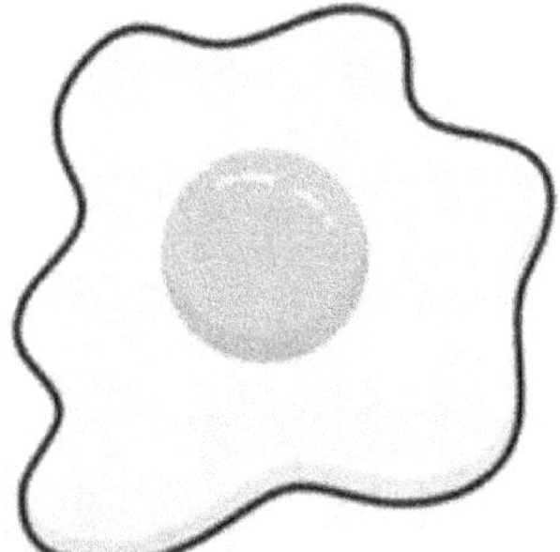

The egg is fried.

beurre

manteiga

The butter is put on bread.

margarine

margarina

Margarine looks like butter.

yaourt

iogurte

That yogurt is popular.

cottage cheese

queijo tipo cottage

The cottage cheese is put on crackers.

crème glacée

sorvete

They have a triple scoop ice cream.

crème

creme

That is a lot of creams.

sandwich

sanduíche

That sandwich is healthy.

saucisse

linguiça

Americans love sausages.

hamburger

hamburger

That hamburger looks happy.

hot-dog

cachorro quente

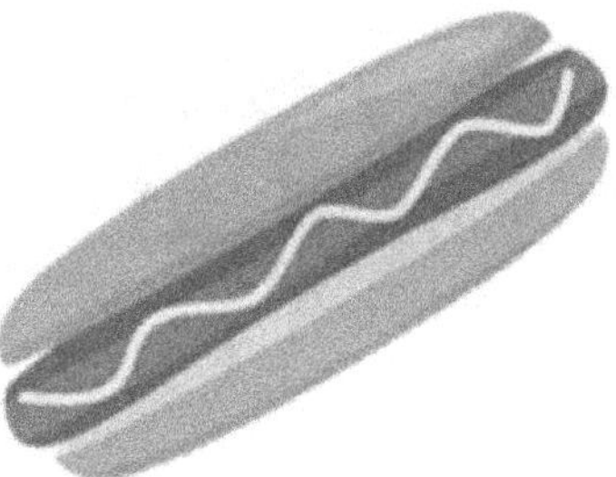

That hot dog has mustard on it.

pain

pão

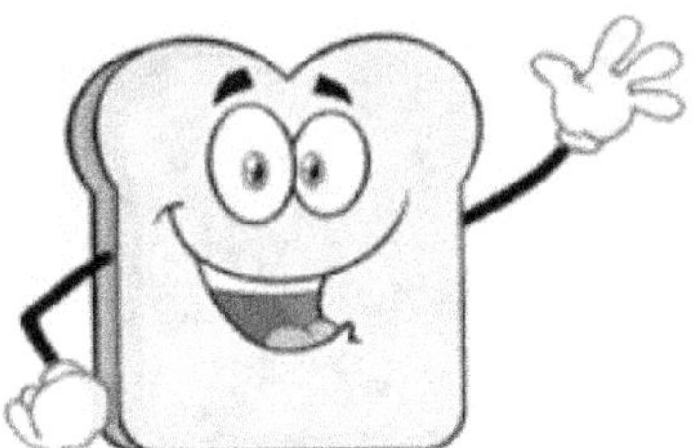

That bread is saying hello.

pizza

pizza

That pizza is cheesy.

steak

bife

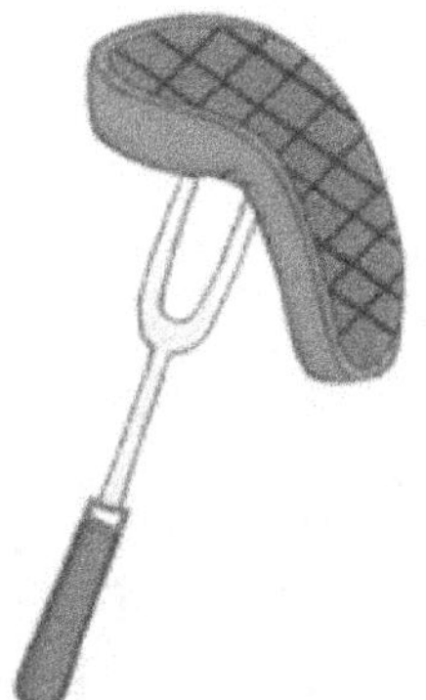

The steak was grilled.

poulet rôti

frango assado

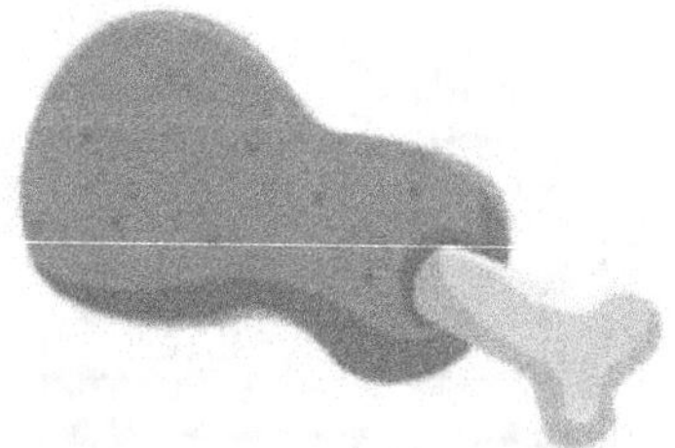

Roast Chicken is delicious.

poisson

peixe

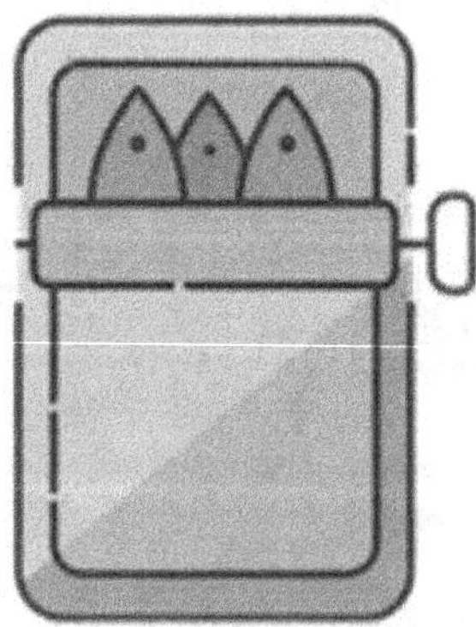

You can buy canned fish in the market.

fruit de mer

frutos do mar

Lobster is expensive seafood.

jambon

presunto

Ham can be put in sandwiches.

kebab

kebab

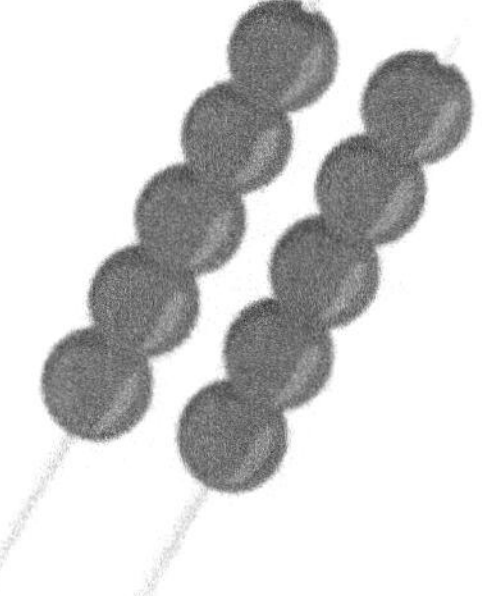

Kebab is a delicacy in America.

bacon

bacon

That bacon is smiling.

crème fraîche

nata

You can dip your chips in sour cream.

vache

vaca

Cows are black and white.

lapin

coelho

That rabbit is fun to play with.

canard

pato

That duck is content.

crevette

camarão

The shrimp has six legs.

porc

porco

That pig is pink and fat.

abeille

abelha

The bee has a stinger.

chèvre

bode

That goat has a white horn.

crabe

caranguejo

The crab has two big pincers.

cerf

veado

That deer is sleeping.

dinde

peru

The turkey has a giant tail.

colombe

pomba

That dove is carrying a plant.

mouton

ovelha

That sheep has fluffy wool.

poisson

peixe

That fish has colorful fins.

poulet

frango

That chicken is waking everybody up.

cheval

cavalo

The horse has a red mane.

chaise

cadeira

That wing chair is yellow.

meuble tv

suporte de tv

The TV stand can hold books.

canapé

sofá

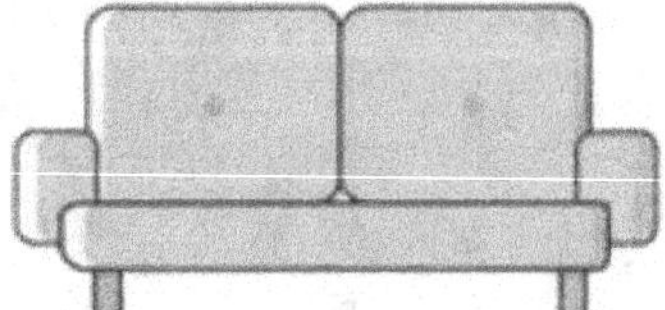

The sofa is comfortable to sit on.

coussins

almofadas

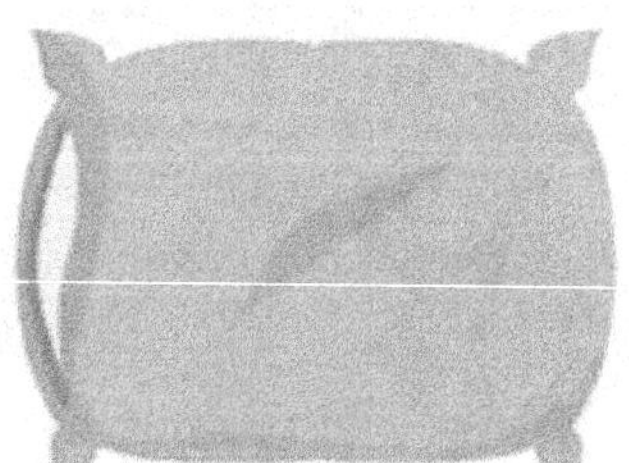

The cushion helps soften your seat.

téléphone

telefone

The telephone is ringing.

télévision

televisão

That television is big.

haut-parleurs

caixas de som

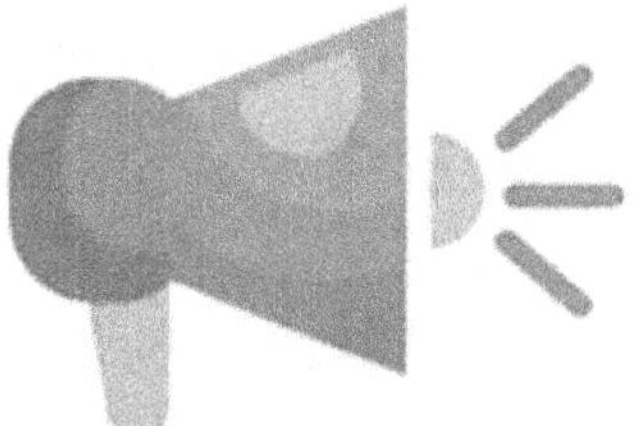

That speaker is used to increase the volume.

table d'appoint

mesa de apoio

That end table is sparkling clean.

service à thé

jogo de chá

That tea set is from China.

cheminée

lareira

The fireplace makes me warm.

télécommandes

remotos

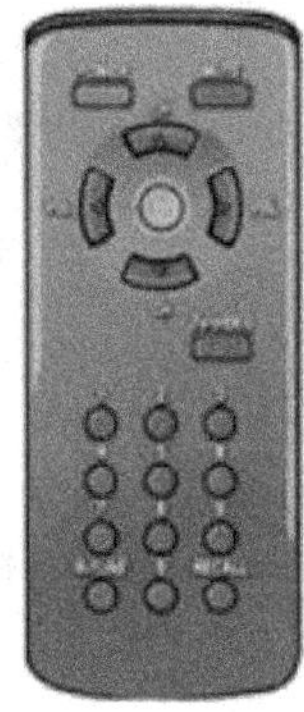

The remote has lots of buttons.

ventilateur électrique

ventilador elétrico

The fan is blowing wind.

lampadaire

luminária de piso

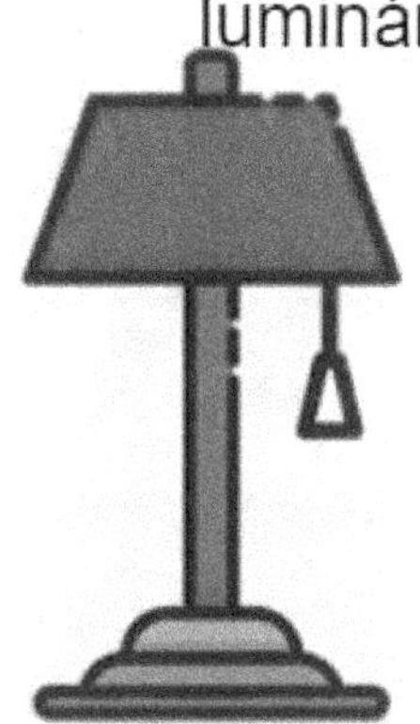

The floor lamp is very tall.

tapis

tapete

The carpet is soft and silky.

bureaux

mesas

The table is made of wood.

stores

cortinas

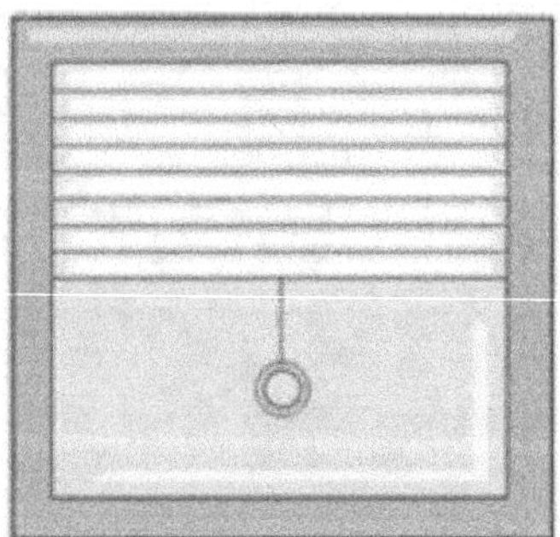

I will pull the blinds down.

rideaux

cortinas

She opened the curtains.

image

cenário

The picture is about the mountains and the sky.

vase

vaso

The roses are all in a vase.

l'horloge

relógio

The alarm clock is beeping.

oreiller

travesseiro

The pillow is pink and yellow.

cintre

cabide de chapéu

The hat stand has only one hat on it.

mettre la table

penteadeira

I have made up on my dressing table.

lampe de table

lâmpada de mesa

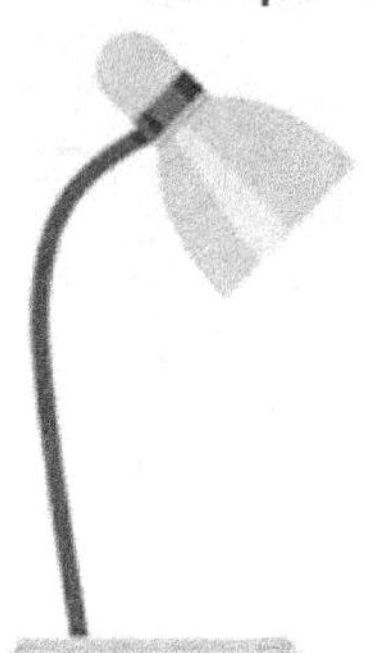

The table lamp will help me see in the dark.

miroir

espelho

The mirror is very tall.

planche a repasser

tabua de passar

Don't touch the ironing board, it's hot!

boîte avec tiroir

caixa com gaveta

You can keep your clothes in the hope chest.

table de chevet

mesa de cabeceira

The nightstand has my lamp on it.

lit

cama

The bed is charming.

climatisation

ar condicionado

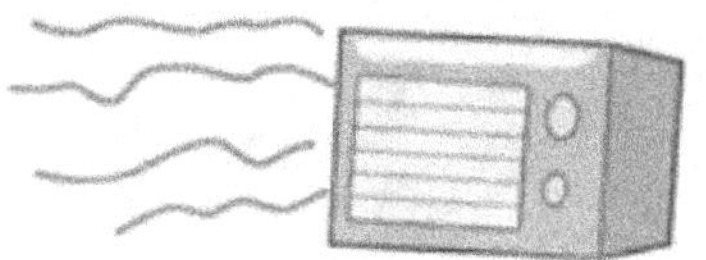

The air conditioner is cold.

cruche

jarro

The measuring jug has nothing inside.

dentifrice

pasta de dentes

The toothpaste is mint flavored.

brosse à dents

escova de dente

The toothbrush has toothpaste on it.

savon

sabonete

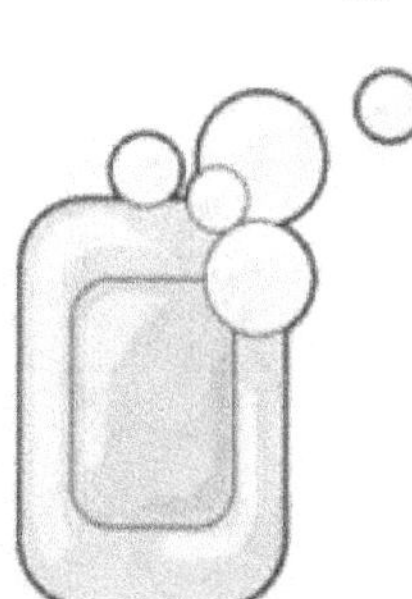

The soap is very bubbly.

pince à linge

prendedor de roupa

The clothespin will clip my clothes.

cintre

cabide

The hanger is hanging my boots.

sèche-cheveux

secador de cabelo

The hairdryer will blow my hair.

shampooing

xampu

The shampoo is used to clean your hair.

bulle

bolha

The bubbles are very fun to play in.

brosse

escova

She is brushing her hair with the brush.

papier toilette

papel higiênico

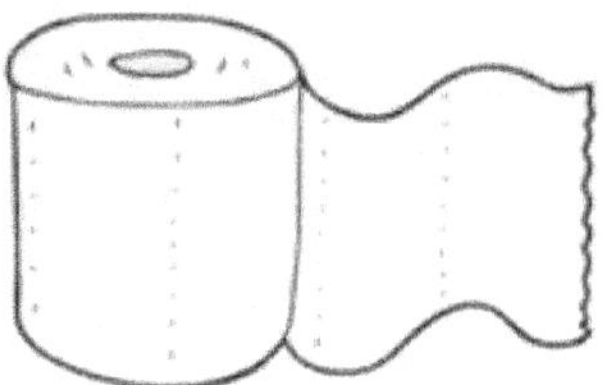

The toilet paper is used to dry your hands.

serviette

toalha

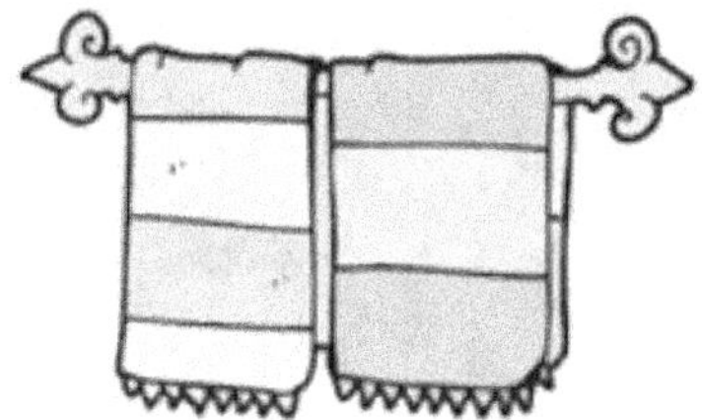

We have two towels on the rack.

corde à linge

varal de roupas

My shirt is hanging on the clothesline.

douche

chuveiro

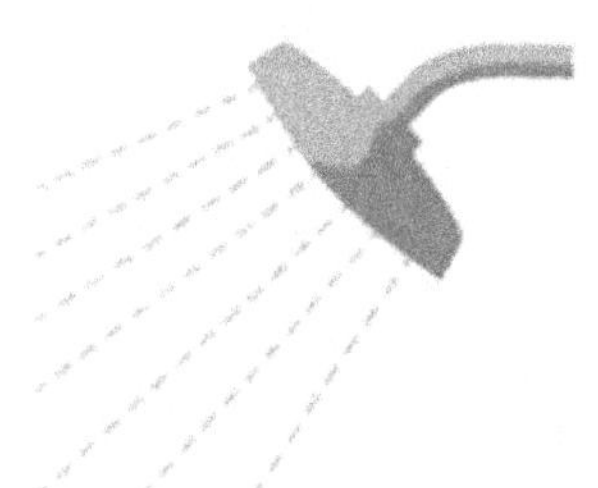

The shower is spraying water.

baignoire

banheira

The bathtub is comfortable.

lessive

detergente para roupa

The laundry detergent is used with the washing machine.

seau

balde

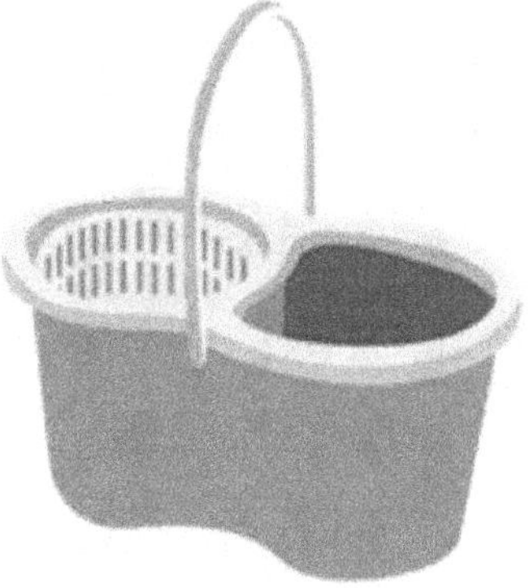

Can you help me fill up the bucket?

vadrouilles

mops

The mop is used for mopping the floor.

savon liquide

sabonete líquido

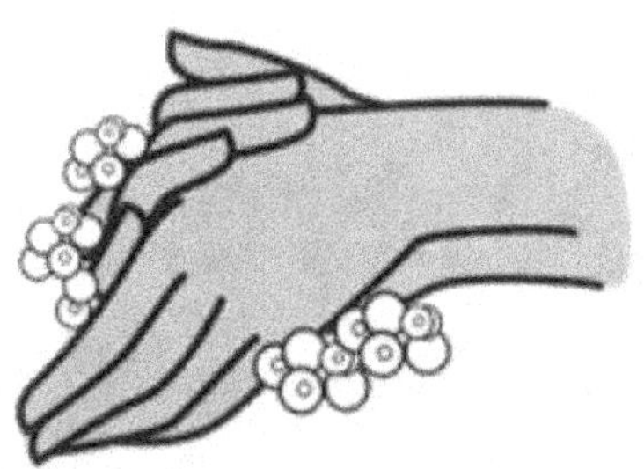

I use soapy water to wash my hands.

lessive en poudre

sabão em pó

I will scoop up the washing powder.

sac poubelle

saco do lixo

The trash bag is full of trash.

poubelle

lixeira

You have only to put recylcle trash in the trash can.

les puits

pias

You should wash your hands in the sink.

cuvette des toilettes

vaso sanitário

She let her bunny use the toilet.

machine à laver

máquina de lavar

The washing machine wash your clothes.

panier à linge

cesto de roupa suja

She is putting all the clothes into the laundry basket.

le rasoir

navalha

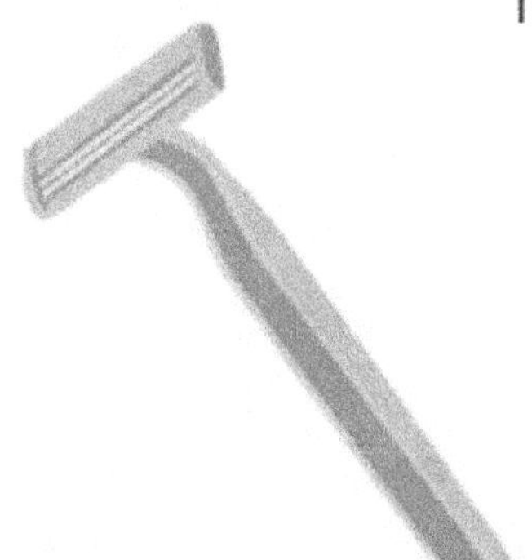

He uses the razor to shave his beard.

rasoir électrique

barbeador elétrico

The electric razor works faster than the normal one.

crème à raser

creme de barbear

The shaving cream is fluffy.

bain de bouche

enxaguatório bucal

The mouthwash smells very lovely.

coton-tige

cotonete

Q-tip can be used for many things.

brosse à cheveux

escova de cabelo

She brushes her hair with her hairbrush.

peigne

pente

Her dad will comb her hair for her.

nettoyant

limpador

Put the cap back on the cleanser bottle.

échelle

escala

You can measure things on the scale.

papier de soie

lenco de papel

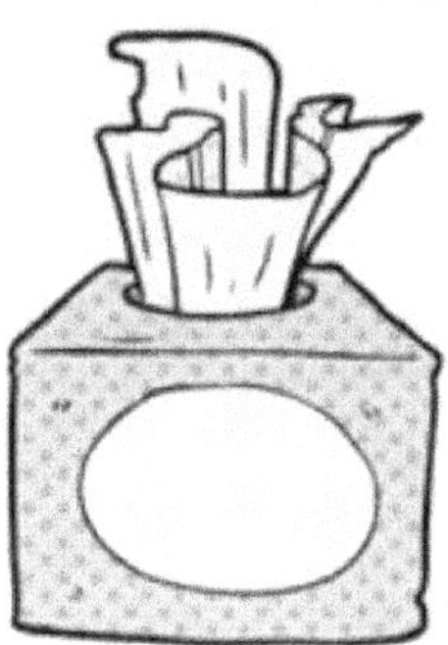

The tissue is on the counter.

jouets de bain

brinquedos de banho

The little duck is a bath toy.

robinet

torneira

The faucet is broken.

miroir

espelho

He is looking in the mirror.

tapis de bain

tapete de banheiro

The bath mat is purple and yellow.